Monitoring Plan for Mercury in Fish Tissue and Water from the Boise River, Snake River, and Brownlee Reservoir, Idaho and Oregon

By Christopher A. Mebane and Dorene E. MacCoy

Prepared in cooperation with the City of Boise

Open-File Report 2013–1068

U.S. Department of the Interior
U.S. Geological Survey

U.S. Department of the Interior
SALLY JEWELL, Secretary

U.S. Geological Survey
Suzette M. Kimball, Acting Director

U.S. Geological Survey, Reston, Virginia: 2013

For more information on the USGS—the Federal source for science about the Earth, its natural and living resources, natural hazards, and the environment—visit *http://www.usgs.gov* or call 1–888–ASK–USGS

For an overview of USGS information products, including maps, imagery, and publications, visit *http://www.usgs.gov/pubprod*

To order this and other USGS information products, visit *http://store.usgs.gov*

Suggested citation:
Mebane, C.A., and MacCoy, D.E., 2013, Monitoring plan for mercury in fish tissue and water from the Boise River, Snake River, and Brownlee Reservoir, Idaho and Oregon: U.S. Geological Survey Open-File Report 2013-1068, 24 p., http://pubs.usgs.gov/of/2013/1068/.

Contents

Tables

Conversion Factors

Multiply	By	To obtain
Length		
inch (in.)	2.54	centimeter (cm)
centimeter (cm)	0.3937	inch (in.)
foot (ft)	0.3048	meter (m)
meter (m)	3.281	foot (ft)
mile (mi)	1.609	kilometer (km)
kilometer (km)	0.6214	mile (mi)
Mass		
ounce, avoirdupois (oz)	28.35	gram (g)
gram (g)	0.03527	ounce, avoirdupois (oz)
gram (g)	0.0001	kilogram (kg)
gram (g)	1000	milligram (mg)
Concentration		
milligram per kilogram (mg/kg)	1	part-per-million (ppm)
microgram per liter (μg/L)	1	part-per-billion (ppb)
microgram per liter (μg/L)	1000	nanograms per liter (ng/L)

Abbreviations

Abbreviation or Acronym	Definition
BAF	Bioaccumulation factor
CRM	Certified reference material
IDEQ	Idaho Department of Environmental Quality
IDFG	Idaho Department of Fish and Game
NPDES	National pollution discharge elimination system
RPTE	Reasonable potential to exceed water quality criteria
TMDL	Total maximum daily load
USEPA	U.S. Environmental Protection Agency
USGS	U.S. Geological Survey

Monitoring Plan for Mercury in Fish Tissue and Water from the Boise River, Snake River, and Brownlee Reservoir, Idaho and Oregon

By Christopher A. Mebane and Dorene E. MacCoy

Abstract

The methylmercury criterion adopted as a water-quality standard in the State of Idaho is a concentration in fish tissue rather than a concentration in water. A plan for monitoring mercury in fish tissue and water was developed to evaluate whether fish in the Boise River, Idaho, upstream and downstream of wastewater-treatment plant discharges, meet the methylmercury water-quality criterion. Monitoring also will be conducted at sites on the Snake River, upstream and downstream of the confluence with the Boise River, and in Brownlee Reservoir, which lies along the border between Idaho and Oregon. Descriptions of standard procedures for collecting and processing samples and quality-assurance steps are included. This monitoring plan is intended to provide a framework for cooperative methylmercury sampling in the lower Boise River basin.

Background and Objectives

Mercury (Hg) is a global pollutant that ultimately makes its way into every aquatic ecosystem through the hydrologic cycle. Atmospheric deposition of inorganic mercury contributes the vast majority of mercury to aquatic systems, although geologic sources and point-source pollution also may contribute to mercury loading. Once inorganic mercury is in aquatic systems, it may become methylated through microbial sulfate reduction (Fitzgerald and Lamborg, 2007). Methylmercury is by far the more bioavailable and toxic form of mercury; and, once mercury has moved through aquatic food chains into predatory fish, almost all mercury present in fish tissue is methylmercury. In turn, game fish that are most commonly caught and eaten in subsistence and recreational fishing tend to be predatory fish. As a result of these dynamics, risks of methylmercury exposure to humans are almost exclusively through consumption of fish (U.S. Environmental Protection Agency, 2011).

Mercury is considered to be a neurotoxin to humans, wildlife, and fish. At the molecular level, mercury is associated with disruptions in the synthesis of selenocysteine, which is one of the 21 amino acids that are essential for all animals. This disruption is related to a cascade of secondary effects from the cellular to the whole organism levels. Other adverse effects associated with methylmercury, such as ionic homeostasis and reactive oxidative stress, are not obviously linked to selenoprotein inhibition. In mammals, including humans, methylmercury has been linked to neurological, cardiovascular, and reproductive impairments. The ability of methylmercury to cross the placental barrier and affect the nervous system of prenatal infants is of greatest concern (Khan and Wang, 2009).

The linkage between mercury and selenium deficiency leads to observations that selenium decreases methylmercury toxicity (Yang and others, 2008; Khan and Wang, 2009). Although much recent toxicological evidence points to the intrinsic linkage of mercury and selenium in their relative risks to humans, wildlife, and fish, recent fish consumption advisories or criteria for protection of human health or the environment have not considered selenium in their assessment of mercury risks (U.S. Environmental Protection Agency, 2001; Idaho Department of Environmental Quality, 2005). Selenium analyses are not included as a required element of monitoring to determine regulatory compliance with methylmercury water-quality criteria in appendix A. However, because (1) the present monitoring plan is expected to persist for several years, obtaining data on selenium residues in fish to accompany the mercury data might have future value in methylmercury risk assessment, and (2) the incremental cost of additional tissue analytes is minor compared to the mobilization and labor costs associated with a sampling program, selenium analyses also are included in the present monitoring plan.

The U.S. Environmental Protection Agency (USEPA) has recommended a water-quality criterion for methylmercury that is expressed as a fish tissue residue value (wet-weight methylmercury in fish tissue). The Idaho Department of Environmental Quality (IDEQ) adopted the USEPA fish-tissue criterion as the State's methylmercury water-quality criterion and published implementation guidance (Idaho Department of Environmental Quality, 2005). The criterion of 0.3 milligrams methylmercury per kilogram (mg/kg) of fresh (wet) weight fish is based on protecting an adult consumer who eats an average of 17.5 grams of fish per day—about one, 8-ounce meal every other week (U.S. Environmental Protection Agency, 2001; Idaho Department of Environmental Quality, 2005). The Idaho implementation guidance document describes two scales of monitoring—facility/source monitoring and statewide ambient monitoring. Facility monitoring provides information about potential sources of mercury, whereas statewide ambient monitoring provides information about impacts of discharges to aquatic life that are tied to total maximum daily load (TMDL) and National Pollution Discharge Elimination System (NPDES) permitting (Idaho Department of Environmental Quality, 2005). However, the statewide ambient monitoring conducted jointly by the U.S. Geological Survey (USGS) and IDEQ was discontinued in 2009 due to fiscal constraints.

The IDEQ guidance document requires NPDES "significant permittees" to provide methylmercury in fish tissue data under the reasonable potential to exceed criteria (RPTE) process (Idaho Department of Environmental Quality, 2005). The RPTE process is designed to protect human health with a fish-tissue methylmercury value not to exceed 80 percent of the 0.3 mg/kg criterion in the receiving water body. Potential mercury dischargers to a water body with fish tissue concentrations >0.24 mg/kg are considered to have a reasonable potential to exceed criteria. In IDEQ's implementation guidance, municipal dischargers are encouraged to establish monitoring cooperatives to help fund watershed-based statewide monitoring for methylmercury in fish tissue. The USEPA further recommended that the permitting authority require only one study per water body (U.S. Environmental Protection Agency, 2010). The monitoring plan presented here is intended to provide a framework for cooperative methylmercury sampling in the lower Boise River basin. A further purpose is to assess compliance with the water-quality criterion for mercury to quantify whether the City of Boise's wastewater discharges appreciably influence fish-tissue mercury concentrations in the lower Boise River and the Snake River upstream and downstream of the confluence with the Boise River. The data also will provide a reference to which future determinations of mercury in fish can be compared.

Project Description

To evaluate whether the Idaho methylmercury fish tissue criterion is being met in the lower Boise River, the USEPA has included mercury sampling requirements for fish tissue and water in the City of Boise's effluent permits for the Lander Street Wastewater Treatment Plant and the West Boise Wastewater Treatment Plant (U.S. Environmental Protection Agency, 2012a, 2012b). The requirements specify that a monitoring plan be written and submitted for approval by USEPA and IDEQ within 1 year of the effective date of the permit. The effective dates of the City's permits are May 1, 2012, through April 30, 2017. The fish-tissue monitoring components of the permits are appended in full in appendix A of this plan and summarized here:

1. Establish six fish-tissue monitoring stations at locations on the Boise River upstream and downstream of the City of Boise wastewater-treatment plants, near the mouth of the Boise River, on the Snake River upstream and downstream of the confluence of the Boise River, and one site in Brownlee Reservoir.

2. Develop a sampling plan that specifies sample target species; sample number and size; timing of sample collection; and all essential fish collection, handling, and shipping information for field sampling teams collecting fish. The plan should include a project description, detailed standard operating procedures (SOPs) for fish collection, and instructions for completing field forms and labels and for shipping fish samples. Protocols should be consistent with Chapter 4 of Implementation Guidance for the Idaho Mercury Water Quality Criteria (Idaho Department of Environmental Quality, 2005).

3. Establish sampling frequency required by the permits to begin within 2 years of May 1, 2012. The monitoring will include three cycles of biennial sampling of five sites, with annual sampling of one site.

4. Present protocols used for preparation of samples and analytical methods and for quality-assurance and quality-control techniques.

5. At each sample location where fish are collected, a surface-water sample must be collected and analyzed for total mercury.

Due to irrigation practices in the lower Boise River basin, fish-tissue sampling is not practical during high flows (May–September). The USGS has conducted previous sampling on the lower Boise River for community assessment and tissue sampling between October 1 and November 30, depending on water levels that, in turn, depend on reservoir and canal operations.

The U.S. Environmental Protection Agency (2012a, 2012b) wastewater discharge permits also call for collecting surface-water samples at each location where fish are collected (appendix A). These water samples are to be processed and analyzed for total mercury in water using an analytical method that achieves a minimum level of 0.5 ng/L (0.0005 µg/L).

The implicit purpose of collecting data on mercury in water and fish tissue at the same location is to facilitate developing fish bioaccumulation factors, which are ratios of tissue and water mercury concentrations. Bioaccumulation factors (BAFs) can be useful for water-quality management, such as site-specific implementation targets of the fish-tissue based methylmercury water-quality criteria, and TMDL target development (Idaho Department of Environmental Quality, 2005; U.S. Environmental Protection Agency, 2010). For developing BAFs, it is not essential that the water and fish samples are collected at the same time. Riva-Murray and others (2012) reported that, in streams in Oregon and New York, the best BAF estimates came from sampling methylmercury in water during the July to September growing season, regardless of when the fish were collected. In related analyses with fish, the optimal approach for estimating BAFs is to use mercury concentration data from at least 10 adult fish of a single species and similar length (Barbara Scudder Eikenberry, U.S. Geological Survey, written commun., 2013).

This monitoring plan is written as if the sampling and analysis methods would all be undertaken by USGS personnel. This is not necessarily the case for a project expected to last more than 10 years. The intent is that the substantive elements of the sampling could be undertaken by any knowledgeable personnel and that the laboratory analyses could be completed by any qualified analytical laboratory that was proficient with comparable methods to those described here.

Monitoring Locations and Frequency

Recent fish-tissue mercury data obtained from within the study area provide background information on the fish species expected at different locations and their tissue mercury concentrations (table 1).

The primary locations planned for collecting fish-tissue samples are listed in table 2. These locations were selected because they were within the broad "upstream of, downstream of" reaches specified by USEPA's permits (appendix A). The USGS also has conducted electrofishing at these locations; thus, some background information on site access and sampling safety is available. Appendix B provides a detailed map of sample sites and their landscape settings.

Sampling must begin in autumn 2013 to meet the deadline outlined in appendix A (within 2 years following May 2012). One site, the Boise River near Middleton, Idaho, downstream of both the Lander and the West Boise Wastewater Treatment Plants, will be sampled each year. The five other Boise River, Snake River, and Brownlee Reservoir sites will be sampled every other year. The frequency of monitoring will follow the rotation listed in table 3.

Target Species

The fish species to be targeted in this monitoring plan are listed in table 4. The selection of target species was based on both the Idaho Department of Environmental Quality (2005) recommendation that fish tissue samples should represent the mercury exposures likely encountered from recreational or subsistence fishing and on the results of previous fish sampling at these locations (table 1; Clark and Maret, 1998; Richter, 2003; MacCoy, 2006). The goal is to collect 10 harvestable-size fish of a target species for individual mercury analysis. Harvestable-size fish are considered to be those fish larger than the minimum lengths for harvest as established by the Idaho Department of Fish and Game (IDFG); or, for fish species without regulatory size limits, individuals greater than 25 cm in length. As of 2013, the minimum harvestable size for smallmouth bass in southwestern Idaho is 12 inches (Idaho Fish and Game, 2013). Thus, for smallmouth bass, the goal will be to collect fish greater than 30 cm in length, rounding to the nearest whole centimeter.

Actually collecting targeted fish species is an inherently uncertain undertaking because species that are common at a location during one sampling event may be scarce or not found during a subsequent event. For making comparisons among sites and over time, it is best to collect samples of similarly sized fish of the same species. However, the inherent variability of fish distribution may make this difficult. Therefore, the sampling crew leader likely will need to make decisions in the field regarding retaining alternate species to only those specified in table 4, retaining 10 harvestable-sized individuals of different species, or moving to another location within the same water-quality reach described in table 2.

Table 1. Selected data for previous mercury in composite fish tissue samples collected by the U.S. Geological Survey in the vicinity of the study area, listed by upstream to downstream sites.

[Data sources: 1997 data are from Clark and Maret (1998); Idaho Department of Fish and Game Nampa Hatchery values are from T. Maret, U.S. Geological Survey, unpublished data; other data are from *http://waterdata.usgs.gov/nwis*. All mercury values are as total mercury; mg, milligram; kg, kilogram; NR, not reported]

USGS site identification	Site name	Year sampled	Species (number analyzed, if specified)	Tissue	Mean mercury (mg/kg wet weight)	Tissue moisture (percent water)
13185000	Boise River near Twin Springs, Idaho	1997	Largescale sucker (7)	Liver	0.23	74
13203760	Boise River at Eckert Road near Boise, Idaho	2011	Mountain whitefish (10)	Fillet	0.15	75.5
13210050	Boise River near Middleton, Idaho	2011	Mountain whitefish (10)	Fillet	0.15	76.5
13213030	Boise River at Mouth near Parma, Idaho	2011	Channel catfish (10)	Fillet	0.23	79.8
13213030	Boise River at mouth near Parma, Idaho	1996	Largescale sucker	Liver	<0.024	76
13172500	Snake River near Murphy, Oregon	2004	Channel catfish (10)	Fillet	0.22	79
13213100	Snake River near Nyssa, Oregon	1997	Channel catfish (8)	Fillet	0.21	77
13213100	Snake River near Nyssa, Oregon	2006	Channel catfish (10)	Fillet	0.22	NR
4422221171355	Brownlee Reservoir at Burnt River, Oregon	1997	Smallmouth bass (6)	Fillet	0.29	79
4422221171355	Brownlee Reservoir at Burnt River, Oregon	1997	White crappie (5)	Fillet	0.27	79
4422221171355	Brownlee Reservoir at Burnt River, Oregon	1997	Channel catfish (7)	Fillet	0.35	75
13211387	IDFG Nampa Fish Hatchery (hatchery reference)	2008	Rainbow trout (5)	Fillet	0.012	75

Because the genesis of this study plan was to evaluate whether the City of Boise's wastewater discharges contribute to an appreciable increase in fish methylmercury concentrations in the lower Boise River, a further target species goal is to collect the same species upstream and downstream of the City of Boise's discharges (table 4, sites 1 and 2). If this is not accomplished during the initial sampling event, the sampling locations should be re-evaluated.

Table 2. Sampling site locations, Boise and Snake Rivers, Idaho, and Brownlee Reservoir, Idaho and Oregon.

[USEPA - U.S. Environmental Protection Agency; RM – approximate river mile upstream of the river mouth. The sampling reaches for boat electrofishing may be up to about a kilometer, and the coordinates are for the approximate center of reach. The coordinates listed in this table may not be identical to the coordinates listed for these sites in NWIS, which usually reflect transects for measuring discharge and or collecting water samples *http://waterdata.usgs.gov*. Coordinates listed in this table are based on WGS84]

Study site No.	USGS site identification	Site name, river mile (RM), and corresponding water quality reach descriptions from the USEPA requirements (appendix A)	North Latitude/West Longitude
1	13203760	Boise River at Eckert Road near Boise, Idaho, RM 58 ("upstream of River Mile 50 in the Lower Boise River")	43°34'07"N, 116° 08'2.04"W
2	13210050	Boise River near Middleton, Idaho, RM 29 ("an area downstream of both of the City of Boise outfalls and near the middle of the Lower Boise River")	43°41'04"N, 116°34'28"W
3	13213030	Boise River at Mouth near Parma, Idaho, RM 2 ("near the mouth of the Boise River")	43°47'52"N, 116°59'41"W
4	13172500	Snake River near Murphy, Idaho, RM 454 ("Snake River upstream of the confluence of the Boise and Snake Rivers")	43°17'31"N, 116°25'12"W
5	13213100	Snake River near Nyssa, Oregon, RM 385 ("Snake River downstream of the confluence of the Boise and Snake Rivers")	43°52'34"N, 116°58'57"W
6	4422221171355	Snake River (Brownlee Reservoir) at Burnt River, Oregon, RM 328 ("within the Brownlee Reservoir")	44°22'22"N, 117°13'55"W

Table 3. Sampling site rotation frequency.

[Study site numbers from table 2. Time of year is for Boise River and Snake River sampling. Brownlee Reservoir sampling may be conducted at different times of the year than other sampling because of safety, coordination with other efforts, to target spring spawning fish aggregations, or other logistical reasons]

Year	Time of year	Study sites to be sampled
2013	October–November	1, 2, 3, 4, 5, 6
2014	October–November	2
2015	October–November	1, 2, 3, 4, 5, 6
2016	October–November	2
2017	October–November	1, 2, 3, 4, 5, 6
2018	October–November	2
2019	October–November	2
2020	October–November	2
2021	October–November	2
2022	October–November	1, 2, 3, 4, 5, 6

Table 4. Target species anticipated at each sampling site, in order of preference for analysis.

[IDFG, Idaho Department of Fish and Game]

Study site No.	Site name	Expected species
1	Boise River at Eckert Road near Boise, Idaho	Mountain Whitefish, Brown Trout, Rainbow Trout
2	Boise River near Middleton, Idaho	Mountain Whitefish, Brown trout, Largemouth Bass, Smallmouth Bass
3	Boise River at mouth near Parma, Idaho	Mountain Whitefish, Largemouth Bass, Smallmouth Bass, Channel Catfish
4	Snake River near Murphy, Idaho	Smallmouth Bass, Largemouth Bass, Channel Catfish
5	Snake River near Nyssa, Oregon	Smallmouth Bass, Mountain Whitefish, Largemouth Bass, Channel Catfish
6	Brownlee Reservoir near Burnt River, Oregon	Smallmouth Bass, Crappie spp., Largemouth Bass, Channel Catfish

Fish collected will be kept in a live well on the boat until they can be weighed and measured. If fewer than 10 harvestable-sized individuals of any game fish species (listed in table 4 or others listed by the IDFG in their annual fishing regulations) can be captured with sufficient effort (defined as a single sampling day for a site), then whatever numbers of harvestable game fish captured will be processed and analyzed. In the event that sampling is compromised, interrupted, or inefficient owing to difficulties such as equipment problems, or if weather or site conditions prevent sampling, additional sampling efforts will be made to collect an adequate sample.

Data-Quality Objectives

The principal data-quality objectives of this sampling and analysis were specified by the U.S. Environmental Protection Agency (2012a, 2012b):

"The objective of the Methylmercury Fish Tissue Monitoring program is to collect reliable methylmercury fish tissue data, within a specific geographic area, to determine if fish tissue concentrations of methylmercury are compliant with Idaho's methylmercury fish tissue criterion of 0.3 mg/kg. The monitoring program may also be used to advise the public on safe levels of fish consumption."

More specific objectives toward meeting those goals include:

1. Fish collections will be designed to collect fish tissue that would be reasonably representative of fish and size ranges likely to be caught and eaten by recreational or subsistence anglers in the vicinity of sampling locations;

2. Sample processing, handling, storing, and shipping to the laboratory will use sufficient quality-assurance measures to avoid introducing sample contamination or bias to the data;

3. Laboratory analytical techniques will be used that have sufficiently low detection limits to quantify Hg levels in fish tissue at less than 0.24 mg/kg wet weight. [The expected laboratory quantification limit for the fish-tissue samples is about 0.005 mg/kg (see section, "Laboratory Methods")].

4. Laboratory analytical techniques will be used that have sufficiently low detection limits to quantify Hg levels in water at 0.5 ng/L.

5. Laboratory analytical techniques will use and report sufficient quality-assurance and control steps that the accuracy and precision of the data reported will be known. The accuracy of the data should be within 20 percent of the most probable value for certified reference materials for mercury in fish tissues, and the precision (repeatability) of the data should be within 20 percent relative percent difference in laboratory replicate analyses.

6. Following review, data will be made available to the public and environmental management agencies through an online database and by periodic data reports.

Field Sampling and Sample Processing

Safety and Crew Training

Although the safety of sampling personnel and bystanders is always a priority during field work, fish collection by boat electrofishing in non-wadeable, flowing water poses real risks of death or injury by electrocution, drowning, or hypothermia. Therefore, appropriate crew training and attention to safety are essential for boat electrofishing. Although it is not feasible to specify all safety precautions in this plan, some key points taken from Meador and Cuffney (1993) and Temple and Pearsons (2007) bear emphasis.

At least one designated crew leader will have received formal training in the principles and safety of electrofishing within 5 years of the sampling event. In addition, crew members will have prior, practical experience in electrofishing and river safety. The training should be acquired through an authoritative source, such as that offered by electrofishing equipment manufacturers. The U.S. Fish and Wildlife Service's National Conservation Training Center (http://nctc.fws.gov/) also provides electrofishing training courses. Before electrofishing begins, the crew leader will be responsible for briefing all crew members on safety precautions.

Maneuvering a boat or raft in a river channel brings inherent risks of capsize or throwing crew members overboard from striking hazards, such as rocks, rubble, rebar, or other debris; becoming entrained in sweepers from downed trees; getting snagged on fencing or tangled in low hanging tree branches; or entrapping feet. Boat work in large waters, such as the Snake River and Brownlee Reservoir in cold weather brings added hazards of hypothermia and swamping from wind waves. These hazards are more acute for an electrofishing crew than for routine recreational boating because of the crew's attention to the operation of the electrofishing unit and spotting and netting fish. Therefore, it is essential that the crew leader is experienced in boat handling, conservative, and does not take avoidable risks. All crew members are responsible for remaining aware of their situation and looking ahead for hazards.

Sampling in the Boise and Snake Rivers will be conducted during periods of low flows, typically October or November, to reduce hazards from maneuvering the boat or raft in high water velocities. Although sampling usually can proceed in mild drizzle or light rain, heavy rain should halt operations. The timing of sampling on Brownlee Reservoir might vary from the river sampling for safety, coordination with other sampling efforts, or to target spawning aggregations. Winds and dangerous waves can come up quickly on a reservoir with a long fetch, such as Brownlee Reservoir. Reservoir sampling and transit will be limited to littoral areas within about 50 m from shore. Insulated float coats that meet U.S. Coast Guard requirements for a Type III personal flotation device (PFD) are recommended in lieu of non-insulated floatation devices for cold-weather river work.

Although electrofishing has been in use for more than 100 years, the application of electricity into water to capture fish is inherently dangerous work, and the voltage and amperage produced by boat electrofishing units is sufficient to electrocute workers (Meador and Cuffney, 1993). Precautions include wearing neoprene waders, rubber lineman-type gloves, and PFDs. Only dipnets with nonconductive fiberglass shafts may be used. The kill switch for the electrofishing unit must be attached to the bow netter, so that if the netter falls overboard, the electrical current will automatically be shut off.

Electrofishing may attract interested bystanders. One crew member should remain onshore and be dedicated to ensuring the safety of bystanders, especially the need to keep children or dogs well clear of the water. A flyer, written in English and Spanish, explaining the purpose and hazards of the sampling would be beneficial to have on hand. If bystanders are likely to be present, dedicating one crew member to public interaction can ensure safety, improve the experience for the public, and allow the other crew members to continue their work without excessive distraction. However, if bystanders do not heed admonitions to stay clear of the water during electrofishing, the sampling must be interrupted. If so, the sampling crew may need to move to a different site or finish sampling at another time.

This summary of some precautions is by no means exhaustive, and is no substitute for actual training and experience. Communication, caution, and situational awareness are essential.

Permits and Coordination

Fish-tissue sample collection requires an Idaho Scientific Collection Permit, which may be granted by IDFG. The permit application is specific to the individual permittee conducting the sampling and to sub-permittees who are qualified to collect in the absence of the permit holder. The permit application also is specific to gear types and to sampling locations. Permit applications must be filed at least 6 weeks prior to planned sampling (http://fishandgame.idaho.gov/public/licenses/). The list of requested sampling locations must be flexible enough to allow for moving the planned sample locations within the general "upstream and downstream of" monitoring reaches listed in appendix A. Sample locations may need to be moved for the safety of sampling personnel or bystanders, or in the event that fishing is poor at a targeted location, or for other operational reasons. For the Brownlee Reservoir samples, any site within the reservoir will be considered to be an acceptable monitoring location. A boat-mounted electrofisher is the preferred method of capture in rivers and near the shoreline in the reservoir, as it involves minimal handling of fish. However, boat electrofishing may not be effective in deep water or for large fish. Therefore, alternate methods, such as gill nets, seines, or hook and line, also should be sought for inclusion in the Idaho Scientific Collection Permit.

Standard Procedures for Sample Collection and Processing

In brief, the procedures for fish sample collection will be as follows:

1. Fish will be collected by electrofishing or alternative permitted methods, and all fish that are eligible for analysis will be retained, alive, in the live well of the boat. This includes all targeted species (table 4) or any fish classified as a game fish by IDFG;

2. When the crew measures the fish, the first 10 fish of the target species listed in table 4 or alternate species, that are greater than 25 cm in length, (except smallmouth bass, which must be greater than 30 cm), may be retained for samples.

3. If enough individuals of the targeted species are not captured within the expected level of effort (one sampling day), then a mixed catch of different species is acceptable. In this event, the crew also will retain samples of any other species listed in table 4 such that a total of 10 game fish greater than 25 cm in length, or for smallmouth bass, greater than 30 cm, were retained;

4. If fewer than 10 individuals of any target fish species greater than 25 cm in length can be caught, then all captured target fish greater than 25 cm in length, or for smallmouth bass, greater than 30 cm, will be retained and processed. All other fish will be released alive, unless specified otherwise in the scientific collection permit.

5. Fish will be individually placed in clean, clear, zip-seal bags on wet ice and returned to the sample preparation area. Fish will be kept on ice and processed within 24 hours to minimize possible loss of sample integrity.

6. Two skinless fillets will be obtained from each fish. One fillet is intended for primary mercury analyses, and the second fillet will be retained frozen as a backup sample. Because the subsamples for selenium will only require about 25 mL of tissue, there will be remaining tissue from the second fillets. The remainder should be retained as a backup sample for up to 6 months (or at least until data reviews are completed) in the event that additional analyses are desired, as a precaution against shipping or other sample mishaps, and as an archive for analytical reruns, if needed.

7. Shipping will be by traceable, overnight delivery service.

More specific details for sample processing are provided in appendix C, which was largely taken from Scudder and others (2008, p. 9-18), following their steps for "Top Predator Fish."

Water samples for analysis will be collected from the same locations as the fish samples, but not necessarily at the same times. If not collected concurrently with the fish samples, the water samples will be collected during the July to September growing season. Water samples will be collected as dip samples for unfiltered, total mercury (UTHg) following the collecting and handling techniques of Lewis and Brigham (2004), or by the functionally similar techniques described by Essig (2010). In short, the technique uses a "clean hands/dirty hands" approach in which one person with clean, powderless gloves handles the sample bottles and the "dirty hands" person assists the clean-hands person by helping them with gloves, opening and sealing bags, and so on. Dip samples will be collected in 500-mL precleaned fluoropolymer or fluorocarbon polymer (FP) bottles. Precleaned FP bottles will be triple-rinsed with the water to be sampled, filled to the shoulder to allow space for preservative, and capped. Samples will be preserved with 10 mL of 6 N ultra-trace hydrochloric acid. Quality-control samples will include at least one field blank per sampling round. A field blank is reagent water that has been transported to the sampling site and exposed to the same equipment and operations as a sample at the sampling site, a procedure defined by Wilde (2006, at section 4.3 "Quality-Control Samples"). Full details on field sampling methods are given by Lewis and Brigham (2004).

Laboratory Methods

Mercury

Biological Total Mercury in Fish Tissue

Although the permit requirements describe a "Methylmercury Fish Tissue Monitoring Program," the laboratory analyses will be for *total* mercury in fish tissue rather than for methylmercury. This is for two reasons: (1) total mercury is easier and less costly for laboratories to determine than is methylmercury, and (2) nearly all mercury present in fish muscle tissue is methylmercury (Bloom, 1992; Hammerschmidt and others, 1999; Harris and others, 2003). Interpretation of total mercury analysis as methylmercury will likely bias high the results as methylmercury in fish on the order of factors of <1.01 to 1.05 based on comparisons shown by Bloom (1992) and by Hammerschmidt and others (1999). This magnitude of potential bias is well within the range of expected analytical variability. In comparing the fish tissue results with the criterion, the analytical results for total mercury in the fish tissue will be interpreted as 100 percent methylmercury.

Analyses of total mercury in fish tissue are planned to be conducted through the USGS Mercury Research Laboratory (USGS MRL), 8505 Research Way, Middleton, Wisconsin, 53562, (608) 821-3844, *http://wi.water.usgs.gov/mercury-lab/*. For "biological total mercury" analyses (that is, of total mercury in fish tissue), the laboratory will provide analyses consistent with USEPA Method 7473 for "Mercury in solids and solutions by thermal decomposition, amalgamation, and atomic absorption spectrophotometry" (U.S. Environmental Protection Agency, 2007).

The biological total mercury method provides a nominal detection limit (minimum level) of 5 ng/g (0.005 mg/kg) dry weight, based on a 20–50 mg sample size. The USGS MRL acceptance criteria for reported data include an acceptable percent recovery on a certified reference material within ±15 percent of the theoretical value, which is more stringent than the overall data acceptance criteria for this overall plan in section, "Data-Quality Objectives." Certified reference materials (CRMs) may include those from the *National Research Council Canada* dogfish liver certified reference material for trace metals or other biological tissues depending on availability, and/or the *National Institute of Standards and Technology (NIST)* Lake Superior or Lake Michigan fish tissue standard reference materials.

The system or method blanks are used to determine the actual detection limits achieved (3X the standard deviation of blanks as mass, then divided by the mass of sample analyzed), which results in the actual detection limits achieved varying sample to sample from the nominal detection limit. The USGS MRL analyzes one sample in triplicate for every 10 samples analyzed, in addition to two system blanks and one CRM. The relative standard deviation of the triplicate analyses (RSD, calculated as the standard deviation/average) should be within 15 percent (John DeWild, USGS Mercury Research Laboratory, written comm., December 5, 2012). Further details of data-quality measures used at the USGS MRL are available online at *http://wi.water.usgs.gov/mercury-lab/index.html*.

As this fish tissue monitoring project matures, different laboratories may be considered for use, depending on factors, such as capacity at the USGS MRL or for the convenience of analyzing both mercury and selenium samples at a single laboratory. Any different laboratories used must meet the *data-quality objectives* specified herein.

Total Mercury in Water

Unfiltered water samples will be analyzed for total mercury using laboratory methods consistent with USEPA Method 1631 (U.S. Environmental Protection Agency, 2002). This method is expected to provide a nominal minimum level of 0.5 ng/L (0.0005 µg/L). Quality-control acceptance criteria for total mercury in water include matrix spikes to determine ongoing precision and recovery, with recoveries within 77 to 123 percent of the theoretical value. The relative percent difference of matrix spike duplicates must be less than 25 percent (U.S. Environmental Protection Agency, 2002). The primary laboratory for the analyses of total mercury in water is anticipated to be the Boise City Water Quality Laboratory, 11818 Joplin Road, Boise, Idaho, 83714. As a contingency, analyses of total mercury in water also may be obtained from Brooks Rand LTD, 3950 Sixth Avenue NW, Seattle, Washington, 98107.

Selenium in Fish Tissue

Because the USGS MRL provides only mercury analyses, analyses for total selenium in fish tissue would be handled by a different laboratory. The specific laboratory has not yet been identified, but it will be expected to provide analyses using modified USEPA Method 1638 (U.S. Environmental Protection Agency, 1996) or alternative methods that provide at least similar performance, such as those of Garbarino and others (2006). Laboratories using this method have obtained minimum levels of 0.1 mg/kg dry weight or less (for example, Essig, 2010). As these analyses are separate from the permit prescriptions for 10-each mercury samples given in appendix A, three samples per site should be sufficient to provide an average value for fish tissue selenium for each site for the species sampled.

Quality Assurance and Quality Control

The sampling and analysis will include both quality-assurance and quality-control measures. Although the concepts of quality assurance and quality control in water-quality monitoring are commonly combined as "QA/QC," the USGS Water Mission Area distinctly defines quality assurance and quality control. *Quality assurance* procedures control those unmeasurable components of a project, such as sampling at the right place with the right equipment and using the right techniques. *Quality control* steps include data generated to estimate the magnitude of the bias and variability in the processes for obtaining environmental data.

Adherence to standard USGS quality-assurance protocols is mandatory, and quality-control procedures are to be incorporated into every water-quality data-collection effort. Quality assurance of the data collected includes the timely and accurate documentation of field information in electronic and paper records, auditing of such records, consistently and conscientiously using procedures and protocols to ensure sample integrity and data quality, and training in measurement techniques and the collection of quality-control data (Wilde, 2009).

Project-specific quality-assurance steps in the field sampling include the use of multiple (10) field replicates to ensure that the samples are representative of that species and size of fish present at the time of sampling, standard procedures for equipment cleaning, sample collection and processing of the field samples, and data reviews. These steps are detailed in their respective sections in this document. Quality-control steps include the analyses of replicates and the use of certified or standard reference fish-tissue sample materials as described in section, "Laboratory Methods."

Reporting

USEPA's permits require that the results must be reported by March 31 of the year following sampling (appendix A). This schedule is feasible if samples can be collected during the July to September sampling index period recommended by the Idaho Department of Environmental Quality (2005) (that is, with a deadline 6 to 8 months post sampling). However, because reservoir and irrigation operations make the Boise River unsafe for electrofishing until October or November annually, this March 31 reporting deadline would only allow 4 to 5 months after the anticipated sample collections for laboratory analyses, data review, and report preparation. Tissue analyses from the USGS MRL in Middleton, Wisconsin may take from 3 to 4 months and subsequent data-quality reviews by the USGS may take up to 2 months. Thus, if fish tissue samples are collected toward the end of November, the final quality-reviewed data may not be available to release online until as late as the end of May and the annual report with the final data by the end of June. To meet USEPA's March 31 reporting deadline under these constraints, we anticipate providing an informal, preliminary sampling completion summary by March 31 of each year, and, as follows, a final data report by June 30 of each year.

Further, to meet the annual reporting requirements of the City of Boise's discharge permits (U.S. Environmental Protection Agency, 2012a, 2012b), a brief annual report will be provided. For the years that seven locations are sampled (table 3), this annual report is expected to be a USGS Data Series report, which is a brief, citable, non-interpretive, online report. Such a report is expected to also satisfy IDFG's required reporting of the fish actually collected through the Idaho Scientific Collection Permit. For the alternate years when only a single site is sampled, the annual report will consist of a simple electronic letter with an attached data spreadsheet.

Additionally, the laboratory data will be stored electronically in the USGS National Water Information System (NWIS), *http://nwis.waterdata.usgs.gov/id/nwis/qwdata*) database and, following review, made publicly available via the NWIS Web Interface. Although this Web address is accurate at the time of writing, as the USGS database is updated and integrated with other databases or data aggregation services, the details of the online data access may change over time.

References Cited

Bloom, N.S., 1992, On the chemical form of mercury in edible fish and marine invertebrate tissue: Canadian Journal of Fisheries and Aquatic Sciences, v. 49, no. 5, p. 1010-1017, http://dx.doi.org/10.1139/f92-113.

Clark, G.M., and Maret, T.R., 1998, Organochlorine compounds and trace elements in fish tissue and bed sediments in the Lower Snake River Basin, Idaho and Oregon: U.S. Geological Survey Water-Resources Investigations Report 98-4103, 35 p. (Also available at http://pubs.er.usgs.gov/publication/wri984103.)

Essig, D.A., 2010, Arsenic, mercury, and selenium in fish tissue and water from Idaho's major rivers: A statewide assessment: Boise, Idaho, Idaho Department of Environmental Quality, 64 p. plus appendixes, accessed September 5, 2013, at http://www.deq.idaho.gov/media/639752-arsenic_mercury_fish_tissue_report_0310.pdf.

Fitzgerald, W.F., and Lamborg, C.H., 2007, Geochemistry of mercury in the environment, in Holland, H.D., and Turekian, K.K., eds., Treatise on Geochemistry: Oxford, Pergamon Press, chap. 9.04, p. 1-47, http://dx.doi.org/10.1016/B0-08-043751-6/09048-4.

Garbarino, J.R., Kanagy, L.K., and Cree, M.E., 2006, Determination of elements in natural-water, biota, sediment, and soil samples using collison/reaction cell inductively coupled plasma—Mass Spectrometry: U.S. Geological Survey Techniques and Methods, book 5, chap. B1, 88 p.. (Also available at http://pubs.usgs.gov/tm/2006/tm5b1/.)

Hammerschmidt, C.R., Wiener, J.G., Frazier, B.E., and Rada, R.G., 1999, Methylmercury content of eggs in yellow perch related to maternal exposure in four Wisconsin lakes: Environmental Science and Technology, v. 33, no. 7, p. 999-1,003, http://dx.doi.org/10.1021/es980948h.

Harris, H.H., Pickering, I.J., and George, G.N., 2003, The chemical form of mercury in fish: Science, v. 301, no. 5637, p. 1,203, http://dx.doi.org/10.1126/science.1085941.

Idaho Department of Environmental Quality, 2005, Implementation Guidance for the Idaho Mercury Water Quality Criteria: Boise, ID, Idaho Department of Environmental Quality, 212 p., accessed September 5, 2013, at*http://www.deq.state.id.us/water-quality/surface-water/mercury.aspx*. .

Idaho Fish and Game, 2013, 2013–2015 Fishing seasons and rules: Website, accessed September 3, 2013, at http://fishandgame.idaho.gov/public/fish/rules/.

Khan, M.A.K., and Wang, F., 2009, Mercury–selenium compounds and their toxicological significance: toward a molecular understanding of the mercury–selenium antagonism: Environmental Toxicology and Chemistry, v. 28, no. 8, p. 1,567-1,577.

Lewis, M.E., and Brigham, M.E., 2004, Low-level mercury, in Wilde, F.D., Radtke, D.B., Gibs, J., and Iwatsubo, R.T., eds., Chapter A5 Processing of Water Samples: National Field Manual for the Collection of Water-Quality Data: U.S. Geological Survey Techniques of Water-Resources Investigations, book 9, accessed December 2012, at http://pubs.water.usgs.gov/twri9A5/.

MacCoy, D.E., 2006, Fish communities and related environmental conditions of the lower Boise River, southwestern Idaho, 1974–2004: U.S. Geological Survey Scientific Investigations Report 2006-5111, 36 p. (Also available at http://pubs.usgs.gov/sir/2006/5111/.)

Meador, M.R., and Cuffney, T.F., 1993, Methods for sampling fish communities as part of the National Water Quality Assessment Program: U.S. Geological Survey Open-File Report 93-104, accessed September 5, 2013, at http://water.usgs.gov/nawqa/protocols/OFR-93-104/.

Moulton, S.R., II, Kennen, J.G., Goldstein, R.M., and Hambrook, J.A., 2002, Revised protocols for sampling algal, invertebrate, and fish communities as part of the National Water-Quality Assessment Program: U.S. Geological Survey Open-File Report 02-150, 75 p. (Also available at http://pubs.usgs.gov/of/2002/ofr-02-150/index.html.).

Richter, T.J., and Chandler, J.A., 2001, Water-level impacts to spawning smallmouth bass, crappie spp., and channel catfish in Richter, T.J., ed., Hells Canyon Complex Resident Fish Study, revised 2003: Boise, Idaho, Idaho Power Company, 76 p., accessed September 5, 2013, at http://www.idahopower.com/pdfs/Relicensing/hellscanyon/hellspdfs/techappendices/Aquatic/e31_05_ch01.pdf.

Riva-Murray, K., Bradley, P.M., Scudder Eikenberry, B.C., Knightes, C.D., Journey, C.A., Brigham, M.E., and Button, D.T., 2012, Optimizing stream water mercury sampling for calculation of fish bioaccumulation factors: Environmental Science & Technology, v. 47, no. 11, p. 5904–5912, http://dx.doi.org/10.1021/es303758e.

Scudder, B.C., Chasar, L.C., DeWeese, L.R., Brigham, M.E., Wentz, D.A., and Brumbaugh, W.G., 2008, Procedures for collecting and processing aquatic invertebrates and fish for analysis of mercury as part of the National Water-Quality Assessment Program: U.S. Geological Survey Open-File Report 2008-1208, 34 p. (Also available at http://pubs.usgs.gov/of/2008/1208/.)

Temple, G.N., and Pearsons, T.N., 2007, Electrofishing: Backpack and drift boat, in Johnson, D.H., Shrier, B.M., O'Neal, J., Knutzen, J.A., Xanthippe, A., O'Neill, T.A., and Pearsons, T.N., eds., Salmonid field protocols handbook: Techniques for assessing status and trends in salmon and trout populations: Bethesda, Maryland, American Fisheries Society, p. 95–132.U.S. Environmental Protection Agency, 1996, Determination of trace elements in ambient waters by inductively coupled plasma — Mass Spectrometry: U.S. Environmental Protection Agency, EPA Method 1638 (SW-846), 50 p.

U.S. Environmental Protection Agency, 2001, Water quality criterion for the protection of human health: methylmercury: Washington, DC, U.S. Environmental Protection Agency, EPA-823-R-01-001, 303 p., accessed September 5, 2013, at http://www.epa.gov/waterscience/criteria/methylmercury/.

U.S. Environmental Protection Agency, Office of Water, 2002, Method 1631, Revision E: Mercury in water by oxidation, purge and trap, and cold vapor atomic fluorescence spectrometry: Washington, D.C., U.S. Environmental Protection Agency, Office of Water, EPA-821-R-02-019, 46 p., accessed September 5, 2013, at http://water.epa.gov/scitech/methods/cwa/metals/mercury/index.cfm.

U.S. Environmental Protection Agency, 2007, Mercury in solids and solutions by thermal decomposition, amalgamation, and atomic absorption spectrophotometry: U.S. Environmental Protection Agency, EPA Method 7473 (SW-846), accessed September 5, 2013, at www.epa.gov/osw/hazard/testmethods/sw846/pdfs/7473.pdf.

U.S. Environmental Protection Agency, 2010, Guidance for implementing the January 2001 methylmercury water quality criteria: U.S. Environmental Protection Agency, EPA-823-R-10-001. 221 p., accessed September 5, 2013, at http://www.epa.gov/waterscience/criteria/methylmercury/.

U.S. Environmental Protection Agency, 2012a, Authorization to discharge under the National Pollutant Discharge Elimination System: Lander Street Wastewater Treatment Facility, City of Boise: U.S. Environmental Protection Agency, Permit No.: ID-002044-3, 53 p., accessed September 5, 2013, at http://yosemite.epa.gov/r10/water.nsf/NPDES+Permits/Current+ID1319.

U.S. Environmental Protection Agency, 2012b, Authorization to discharge under the National Pollutant Discharge Elimination System: West Boise Wastewater Treatment Facility, City of Boise: U.S. Environmental Protection Agency, Permit No.: ID-002044-3, 52 p., accessed September 6, 2013, at http://yosemite.epa.gov/r10/water.nsf/NPDES+Permits/Current+ID1319.

Wilde, F.D., ed., 2006, Collection of water samples: U.S. Geological Survey Techniques of Water-Resources Investigations, book 9, chap A4 (v. 2.0), 231 p., accessed September 5, 2013, at http://water.usgs.gov/owq/FieldManual/chapter4/html/Ch4_contents.html.

Wilde, F.D., 2009, Guidelines for field-measured water-quality properties: U.S. Geological Survey Techniques of Water-Resources Investigations, book 9, chap A6 (v. 2.2), (Also available at http://pubs.water.usgs.gov/twri9A5/.)

Yang, D.-Y., Chen, Y.-W., Gunn, J.M., and Belzile, N., 2008, Selenium and mercury in organisms: Interactions and mechanisms: Environmental Reviews, v. 16, p. 71-92, http://dx.doi.org/10.1139/A08-001.

Appendix A. Excerpt of U.S. Environmental Protection Agency Permit No.: ID-002398-1 Requirements for Methylmercury Fish Tissue Monitoring (U.S. Environmental Protection Agency, 2012a, p., 19–20)

Methylmercury Requirements

1. Fish Tissue Sampling

Objective: The objective of the Methylmercury Fish Tissue Monitoring program is to collect reliable methylmercury fish tissue data, within a specific geographic area, to determine if fish tissue concentrations of methylmercury are compliant with Idaho's methylmercury fish tissue criterion of 0.3 mg/kg. The monitoring program may also be used to advise the public on safe levels of fish consumption.

Applicability: The permittee may satisfy the requirements of the Methylmercury Fish Tissue Monitoring Program by arranging to participate in a cooperative effort with other entities which have NPDES permitted discharges to the Lower Boise River or tributaries to the Lower Boise River.

Requirements: The permittee must develop and submit a Methylmercury Fish Tissue Monitoring Plan to the Director of the Office of Water and Watersheds and the IDEQ for review and approval within one year of the effective date of the permit. At a minimum the plan must include the following elements:

- Identify all participants (e.g., City of Boise, other municipalities or industries) funding the monitoring program. The monitoring plan must be updated each time a municipality or industrial facility joins the cooperative monitoring program, and the City of Boise must provide notice to the USEPA and the IDEQ each time a new entity becomes part of the cooperative monitoring program. Written notice must be provided to the USEPA and the IDEQ within 30 days of a new participant joining the program.
  - Monitoring stations where fish tissue samples will be collected. One monitoring station must be located in each of the following areas:
    - Upstream of River Mile 50 in the Lower Boise River
    - An area downstream of both of the City of Boise outfalls and near the middle of the Lower Boise River
    - Near the mouth of the Boise River
    - Snake River upstream of the confluence of the Boise and Snake Rivers
    - Snake River downstream of the confluence of the Boise and Snake Rivers
    - Within the Brownlee Reservoir
  - Name, address of organization collecting and analyzing fish tissue samples. The organization must have experience in the collection and analysis of methylmercury fish tissue samples.

- Develop a sampling plan that specifies sample target species, sample number and size, timing of sample collection, and all essential fish collection, handling, and shipping information for field sampling teams collecting fish. The plan should include a project description, detailed standard operating procedures (SOPs) for fish collection, and instructions for completing field forms and labels and for shipping fish samples. Protocols should be consistent with Chapter 4 of Implementation Guidance for the Idaho Mercury Water Quality Criteria (Idaho Department of Environmental Quality, 2005).
- Identify all protocols related to sample preparation methods and analytical methods to be used on samples.
- Identify data quality goals for all sample collection and handling activities and describe the Quality Assurance/Quality Control (QA/QC) techniques employed by field teams to support those goals.

Sample Frequency: Initial sampling must occur within 2 years of the effective date of the permit. Following the initial sampling event monitoring must occur at least once every two years from five of six sample locations, and yearly at the sixth location. After three sampling cycles, five of the six sample locations should be sampled once every 5 years. Sample sites will be determined in consultation with IDEQ.

Additional Sampling: At each sample location where fish are collected a surface water sample must be collected and analyzed for total mercury using an analytical method which achieves a Minimum Level of 0.0005 µg/L.

Reporting Requirements: The permittee must submit a report which lists the participants financing the monitoring program; the name, address and phone number of the entity collecting and analyzing samples; sample locations; target species used; sample size; time samples were collected; analytical methods used; results, and any other information relevant to the monitoring program. The permittee must submit the report to the USEPA, the IDEQ and the Idaho Fish Consumption Advisory Board by March 31st of the year following sampling.

Revision to the Methylmercury Monitoring Plan: Any revisions to the Methylmercury Monitoring Plan must be approved by the IDEQ and the Director of the Office of Water and Watersheds.

Appendix B. Map of Study Sites

Appendix B is online only, and consists of a detailed map of sample sites and their landscape settings, viewable with the Google Earth application (http://www.google.com/intl/en/earth/index.html) or other Internet-based, two-dimensional map and three-dimensional Earth browsers (.kml file). The .kml file can be downloaded at http://pubs.usgs.gov/of/2013/1068/.

Appendix C. Standard Operating Procedures for Fish Collection and Processing

The following procedures were excerpted from Scudder and others (2008), omitting some internal citations.

Preparation of Equipment and Supplies

Suggested equipment and supplies are listed in appendix 2 of Scudder and others (2008). Supplies and equipment that come in contact with organisms should consist of new or clean plastic (Teflon®, polypropylene, polyethylene, or polyethylene terephthalate whenever possible). When in doubt, consult the USGS MRL in Middleton, Wisconsin regarding container recommendations. High-grade stainless steel knives may be used for filleting and dissecting fish.

Prepare assembled equipment and supplies to minimize the potential for sample contamination. New, sealed supplies, such as zip-seal plastic bags and plastic vials with plastic caps, do not need pre-cleaning for the purposes described in this biological sampling protocol. Prior to field work, clean all other supplies and equipment in a dilute (0.1-percent by volume) solution of non-ionic surfactant detergent (Liquinox®) by soaking equipment for 30 minutes and then using a plastic scrub brush to scrub all surfaces. Rinse equipment with copious amounts of tap water because residual detergent on supplies or equipment could contaminate tissues for stable carbon isotope and other chemical analyses. All non-metal equipment (for example, cutting boards, trays, plastic forceps, plastic sieves) should then be soaked in 5-percent hydrochloric acid (trace metal grade such as Omni Trace®) for 8 to 24 hours prior to initial sampling and triple rinsed in deionized (DI) water (<0.055 µS/cm). Fillet knives and other stainless steel tools should not be cleaned with acid; these tools should be cleaned with dilute detergent solution, rinsed with copious amounts of tap water, triple rinsed with DI water, and air dried completely prior to storage in order to minimize corrosion. Small, high-grade stainless steel disposable dissecting knives are an option for processing forage fish. After they are cleaned, supplies and smaller equipment should be double-bagged in new, clear plastic bags and stored in sealed containers to minimize contamination; supplies should be cleaned and packed separately for each site to minimize the need for field cleaning. Large, new, clear plastic bags can be used to wrap nets and other gear so that they do not directly contact truck beds or other potentially highly contaminating surfaces. In the field, all equipment should be cleaned between sites by scrubbing with dilute Liquinox® and rinsing with copious amounts of tap water, triple rinsing with DI water, rinsing with 5-percent hydrochloric acid (non-metal items only), and again triple rinsing with DI water.

Preparation and Review of Field Forms and Labels

Field personnel should preview field forms, sample labels, and laboratory submission forms. See section on Field Data Forms and Sample Labels later in this appendix. Examples of completed forms and labels are provided by the USGS MRL. Field forms and labels should be preprinted with station name, USGS station number, analyte, medium code, and contact information for the project chief (name, e-mail, and telephone number). This is not only a valuable time-saving measure for field work but an important tool for to minimizing errors on field forms.

Fish Collection

Fish may be collected by any means that do not result in contamination of their tissues for chemical analyses. A variety of fish-collection procedures may be appropriate, depending on site conditions and target species. General fish-collection procedures are described elsewhere (Meador and Cuffney, 1993; Moulton and others, 2002), and rely primarily on electrofishing (backpack, barge, and boat). Other methods in combination with or in lieu of electrofishing, such as seining or rod-and-reel (with artificial lures), or passive gear, such as traps or nets, may be more effective at some sites and are acceptable. After capture, fish should be placed in a live cage/net in the stream (large top predator fish only, as small forage fish may be damaged), a large aerated bucket, or an aerated live well to minimize stress until processing, to keep fish alive, and to allow any unneeded fish to be returned live to the stream. Fish can be anesthetized using carbon dioxide from carbon dioxide-producing tablets, such as Alka-Seltzer® (2-4 tablets per gallon of water in bucket or other container). After anesthetization, fish can be euthanized by additional carbon dioxide or a sharp blow to the base of the skull. If fish are to be processed in a location other than where they were collected, place them in clean zip-seal bags on wet ice and process them within 24 hours to minimize possible loss of sample integrity.

Sample Processing

Samples must be processed in a clean environment. Processing at the site, or a nearby outdoor area, is acceptable if a stable, clean work area is available. Processing in an enclosed facility, such as a field laboratory, also is acceptable. Avoid sources of contamination, such as dusty roads, heavy traffic, older field and laboratory vehicles, or older buildings where dust and (or) particle-shedding from building materials (for example, paneling, or ceiling tiles) might be of concern. Avoid facilities or vehicles where any forms of Hg, including Hg-based preservatives and manometers, have been used. Cover all work surfaces with new clear plastic sheeting or bags. Wear disposable, powder-free plastic gloves during all sample processing. Change gloves frequently, particularly after touching any unclean surface. Clean, thicker reusable plastic gloves, such as dishwashing gloves, may be used for fish handling where thinner, disposable gloves would tear upon contact with spines of a fish. For reusable gloves, wash outsides thoroughly with detergent solution, tap water, and DI water between sampling sites.

Care should be taken during sample processing and storage to minimize desiccation as fish contain approximately 75 to 80 percent water (for example, table 1). Low sample weights resulting from desiccation will bias the calculation of "wet-weight" Hg concentrations from reported dry-weight values. Therefore, the smallest appropriate sample container should be used, and all air expressed from zip-seal bags when used. Processed samples should be preserved immediately on dry ice for transport to a freezer or analytical laboratory and analyzed as soon as possible, preferably within 6 months. Scudder and others (2008) illustrate fish processing steps with detailed illustrations and close-up photographs, which we have not attempted to reproduce here.

Field Data Forms

Labeling the sample properly and filling out all field forms and other paperwork correctly and completely are critical steps in ensuring proper data management. Blank field forms are available for *analytical services requests* and *cooler inventory forms* are available online from the USGS MRL. Examples of acceptable field data forms and sample analytical service requests follow:

FIELD DATA SHEET (NWIS field name noted in parentheses)										
USGS Mercury studies--Fish tissue samples						Project:				
Station Name (SNAME):										
Station ID (STAID):					Sample date (DATES), YYYYMMDD:					
Time range, 24h, HHMM -HHMM:						Medium Code (MEDIM): **C**				
Sample Type (STYPE): **H**			Analysis status (ASTAT): **ME**			Hydrologic condition (HSTAT): **A**				
Field Crew:										
Field comments:										
Species Common name:						Latin name:				
ITIS Taxonomic code (TAXON):						Body part code (BDPRT):				

Fish #	Sample time (TIMES) *(24 h)*	Fish length, total, cm, P91106	Fish wt, g, P91104	Sample wt, g, P91105	Gender, Male, P47463	Gender, Female, P47462	Scale/ Otolith	Sample ID	NWIS Record #
1									
2									
3									
4									
5									
6									
7									
8									
9									
10									
11									
12									
13									
14									
15									

USGS Mercury studies--Fish tissue samples

Study Unit contact:
Phone number:
Shipped by:
Shipping date:
Received by:
Received date:

Shipper instructions:

(1) Save a COPY of this form
(2) Enter sample data into this spreadsheet
(3) Sign, date, and ship hard copy of completed form with samples
(4) Email electronic copy to laboratory to facilitate lab log-in.

Lab Instructions:

(1) Sign, date, and note comments upon receipt of samples.
(2) Save form. Fax or mail copy to Study Unit contact.

Study Unit (SU) notes to lab:

Analyses requested: *Total Mercury*   Medium Code: C

Lab notes / condition of samples:

Sample data

STAID	DATES	TIMES (24 h)	Species	Fish length, total (cm)	Fish wt (g)	Sample Cut	Sample wt (g)	Gender (M/F/I)	Sample ID	Comments

Sample Shipment

Before shipping the samples, verify that the samples have been recorded on appropriate sample submissions forms and call the analytical laboratory to confirm that the laboratory is prepared to properly receive the samples. Frozen samples must be express-shipped (next-day delivery), and must contain sufficient dry ice so that a 1-day delay in delivery (due to weather, for example) will not compromise sample integrity. Up to 2.5 kg of dry ice generally can be shipped by air express in non-airtight (vented) coolers without requiring Hazardous Material Agreements or incurring additional costs. Coolers with dry ice can not be airtight, require a dry ice placard, and labeling, depending on the shipper's practices. Contact the shipper for specific instructions. Samples should be shipped on Mondays or Tuesdays to lower the risk that frozen samples will sit for days while enroute to the laboratory. Notify the laboratory that samples have been shipped and request a notification of receipt if one is not automatically provided by the laboratories.

Paper copies of completed laboratory submission forms must accompany sample shipments. In addition to paper copies of laboratory submission forms, submit electronic copies to the appropriate laboratory to facilitate data management. Copies of all forms and record sample shipment date and, if available from the shipping company, the tracking number for each shipment must be retained.

Data Review and Release

Upon receipt from the laboratory, data will be reviewed by USGS staff. Generally the data will be entered into the USGS *National Water Information System* by the laboratory, but if not, it will be the responsibility of USGS Idaho Water Science Center staff to do so. Data will be coded as provisional until quality reviewed. The review will include at least the following checks:

- Are the site identification, sample media type, species, and Integrated Taxonomic Information System (*www.ITIS.gov*) codes correct?
- Do the reported results appear reasonable based on previous data at the site or species? Is the correct parameter code (63792, at the time of writing) for total mercury in fish tissue used? Are data from field replicate samples stored under the same site and parameter code and same sample date?
- Is the relative percent difference between replicate analyses of laboratory split samples >50 percent? If so, the data should not be used for any purpose and should be rejected from the database.
- Is the relative percent difference between laboratory replicate samples >20 percent and <50 percent? If so, the data will be published, but must be flagged as not meeting quality-control objectives.
- Was recovery of mercury or selenium from certified reference materials within ±20 percent of expected values?
- Can data conversions from dry weight to wet weight be reproduced?